CONTENTS

CHAPTER 1

GETTING STARTED

Congratulations on taking the first step towards your financial success. Success within any endeavor always begins with education. Getting started with your financial education will bring you confidence in your decision-making, but most importantly, being financially sound brings you peace of mind.

Why are we talking to each other, and why should you listen to me? I can only assume you picked up this book because there is something that you desire for yourself that is currently missing. Most likely, there is a desire for a better "future self" that you have in mind. Our journey through this book will center around lifestyle design. *Lifestyle design* is the perfect word-play for someone seeking a better future. It is all about creating the life you desire.

If *you* don't design your life, someone else will!

There are certainly many facets to lifestyle design. Within my practice, we focus on three primary areas of lifestyle design. We focus on being relationally rich, physically fit and financially free. This book will focus on the latter, which is centered around making the best financial decisions possible. When you get your money right, a lot of other tensions or problems seem to disappear.

IF YOU
DON'T
DESIGN
YOUR LIFE,
SOMEONE ELSE
WILL!

Chapter 2

ABOUT ME

My career began back in 1997, in a very traditional insurance agency(ish) financial firm. This was a perfect complement to my college career, which focused on economics and marketing. Having always enjoyed the study of money, stocks, bonds and the like, I desired to create a more well-rounded practice after 12 years of literally gaining the best financial education possible. I am grateful to the many mentors I had along the way.

Several years later, I noticed that my new practice was doing a great job at making people wealthy; however, there was something majorly wrong. The individuals we were serving, and serving well, weren't always happy people. As a Christian, I inherently knew there was more to life than money, but sadly, most people I was serving were not seeking success outside of money.

A new direction was established! Drive Planning was designed with the end user, our client, in mind. It doesn't and shouldn't seem revolutionary when you say this aloud. However, a majority of firms are designed around rules, regulations and profits. I desired an environment to help individuals, couples and business owners to be truly successful. Honestly, I didn't know the term *lifestyle design* when we first got started years ago. Our process was designed to be intentional (which is now a buzzword, and I'm not claiming credit for it). Simply put, our new vision was to direct and guide people towards true success, which we defined as being relationally rich, physically fit and financially free. I figured if a person got those right, they were going to lead a really good life.

THE PROTECTION SAVINGS
AND GROWTH MODEL

PS&G Model® Present Financial Position

Date
Last Name

First Name	Age
Client	
Spouse	
Child	
Child	
Child	
Child	

Occupation	Income
Client	
Spouse	

Total Income $ _____

% of Income Saved _____ %

Additional Information

Debt Window

Type of Loan	$/Month Principal & Interest	$ Unpaid Balance	% Rate	Months to Pay

Vehicle Insurance	Property Insurance	Liability Insurance
Disability Insurance	Medical Insurance	Government Plans
Wills & Documents	Trusts & Ownership	Life Insurance

Regular Savings	Credit Union	Time Deposits
Savings Bonds	Certificates	Money Market
Tax Deferred	Tax Free	Tax Deductible

Government Bonds	Corporate Bonds	Municipal Bonds
Preferred Stocks	Bluechip Stocks	Growth Securities
Collectibles	Real Estate	Tax Shelters

IMPORTANT: Read reverse side   WS001-INT-R0702

CHAPTER 3

IDEOLOGY

I f you have the proper ideology, much of the battle is won (if you don't, it is unfortunately lost). Ideology in this context means having the proper mindset or thoughts about money. Much of what we believe about money is learned from our parents. It seems like the older a person gets, the more like their parents they become. In a few rare cases, we see individuals who turn in the opposite direction and avoid, at all cost, the path of their parents. Either way, it is learned from their parents.

We are often taught that debt is _____ and that cash is _____. I suspect that you by nature inserted the words *bad* and *king* respectively. We all have been taught these things, and they are radically untrue. Common parental advice tells us that we should go to school and get a good education so we can get a good Job. Yet, most Americans admire the owner or the boss and more millionaires are created out of real estate than anything else. It is counterintuitive to work towards a job.

The first step in your success journey should always begin with assessing your hopes and dreams and with defining what you want out of life. If you're going to design your life, don't shoot low! I suspect that as a kid, you didn't daydream about being a middle manager! So, this is the time to think BIG. Do not allow your learned or limiting beliefs define you. Break the mold.

The latter half of the hopes and dreams exercise is identifying major roadblocks that could prohibit you from achieving the success you desire. As we think about roadblocks, we must identify the life-altering dream destroyers.

This book will follow the philosophy of the Lifetime Economic Acceleration Process (LEAP), which I have used since 2001. The LEAP founder, Robert Castiglione, designed the process to be economics-based, eliminating undo bias from any financial institution. The process stresses the importance of using the proper financial tools to rapidly accelerate or multiply your wealth. Our goal will be to create cash flow, but not to accumulate excessive cash reserves. Cash reserves are like sitting ducks waiting to be obliterated through taxes, market loss, inflation or lawsuit.

At some point in your life, you probably played a board game like Monopoly. You rolled the dice and followed the track around the board. The path was easy to understand and the moves to make were clearly defined, but what if you pulled the board away and were only left with the pieces? Now, it wouldn't be so easy to understand. Where do you go? What's your next step? I see people every day who try to tackle their personal finances without the "gameboard." No model = chaos. The PS&G Model will serve as the gameboard for viewing our financial life and literally following the rules or process, which will tell us what to do next.

In the coming chapters, we will look inside of the areas of the financial model and discuss the major points to identify and the pitfalls to avoid. My career has afforded me the luxury of working with the young and old, the super-rich and those just getting started, with many facets in between.

We can't change the past, but we can change how we move forward. The model will serve as our guide.

CHECKING UNDER THE HOOD

Much like a mechanic would do if trying to diagnose problems with a vehicle, when getting started with your financial plans, it's good to check for leaks. Leaks in a financial sense is money that is being lost either unknowingly or unnecessarily. Far too often, we see other advisors whose sole focus is getting a larger return on your money. It is certainly important to get a good return, but it is more important to consider the efficiency of your decisions.

For example, you wouldn't want to continuously have to put fuel into your vehicle while ignoring the hole in your gas tank. I'll spare you further analogies because I feel certain you get the picture.

Where should you begin to search for financial leaks? Just like you'd probably go to a mechanic/technician if looking to diagnose a problem with your automobile, I'd recommend visiting a professional to assist you in your planning. In fact, I'd suggest you visit a team of professionals since specialties differ in the financial field.

With your visibility of your personal finances improving due to your newfound modeled approach, you should begin, either on your own or together with your team, to look in the 5 key areas where we always find the most waste:

1. How to pay for taxes
2. How to fund a retirement plan
3. How to pay for your home (or wherever you sleep)
4. How to pay for education (either yours or your children's)
5. How to make major purchases (cars, vacations, investments, the *big* stuff)

You are well equipped with a financial model/gameboard, and now you know exactly where to look for the big issues. My goal is to further equip you with loads of tips and recommendations. However, I still believe you should work with professionals to assist you on the journey.

A GUIDE IS HELPFUL, ESPECIALLY WHEN YOU'VE NEVER BEEN THERE BEFORE.

I can appreciate the DIY approach for some projects; however, I don't believe this is the time to get overzealous in your abilities. Many of the wealthiest people in the world have a team of advisors whom they look to for guidance. Famous real estate investor and *Rich Dad, Poor Dad* author, Robert Kiyosaki, is one of the most notable for talking about his team of financial advisors. Many billionaires discuss their ideas with teams of advisors.

You may be thinking at this point, "Sure, but wealthy people can afford those advisors." Allow me to let you in on a little secret: if properly chosen, a team of financial advisors will make you money, NOT cost you money!

Our team of advisors consists of planners, accountants, tax strategists, insurance specialists, portfolio managers, real estate agents/pros, marketing professionals and more—a group of specialized and handpicked professionals all working for you. You may be thinking, "Wait, Todd, I already have all of those people." It is highly likely that you do; however, I would ask, "How often do they all meet and discuss your hopes and dreams? Have they ever even asked you about your hopes and dreams? A gentleman told me years ago that the only time all those people are together in the same room is at your funeral. I certainly hope not because coordination between all these specialists is integral to achieving your life goals.

In the coming chapters, we will walk through the PS&G Model. Together, we will explore some of the technical matters to consider. Onwards, we go!

CHAPTER 4

HOW MUCH?

The proper answer to this question is, "As much as possible." But wait, we didn't clarify. How much of what? Related to money and our personal finances, I still believe that I have the answer correct (about 99% of the time), regardless of the actual question. Let me explain.

If the question is, how much should I invest every month? "As much as possible" is the correct answer. If the question is, how much money will I need? Again, as much as possible. How much insurance should I have? As much as possible. How much should I save? Now, let's talk serious because that isn't the proper answer any longer.

HOW MUCH SHOULD I INVEST?

The quick answer to this question is 15% of your income. This isn't a number that I arbitrarily created. There are economic factors that dictate this being the necessary amount to put away in order to simply maintain status quo. Factors such as the ones listed below dictate our minimum rate to invest:

- Planned obsolescence: Things will need replacing, such as lightbulbs, cars, and equipment.
- Taxes: Self-explanatory.
- Technology: There will always be new technology that we will consume.
- Inflation: The currency today will not purchase as much in the future.
- Lost-opportunity costs: Money we use to consume goods and services doesn't stay within our financial system to produce cash flow in the future.

HOW MUCH MONEY WILL I NEED IN THE FUTURE?

As much as possible! Always plan for maximum output. Many advisors suggest using mathematical equations to predict a rate of return and duration of time. I want to try and get the most money possible. This is done by creating a diligent and intentional approach towards your financial life. Follow the rules laid out in this book, and you will get there.

Striving for the maximum income is necessary because our hopes and dreams typically expand as we age. Living a full life will almost always create more opportunities to give and to serve others. There will likely be people in your future you will want to generously provide for that you haven't even met yet. Think kids, grandkids and charities for starters. When you dream properly, you don't dream in minimal terms.

HOW MUCH SHOULD I SAVE?

Maybe by now you have noticed that I've avoided using the term *save* or *saving*. Saving should be limited to your emergency reserves. Saving dollars will not get you ahead. Inflation and other wealth devastators make saving money a losing strategy. As you'll see in the pages ahead, our focus will be on creating cash flow.

"Savers are losers." - *Robert Kiyosaki*

CHAPTER 5

PROTECTION

Years ago, I took a trip down the Rhine River in Germany. It was a beautiful experience to see all the castles along the riverbanks. Many of these ancient, giant fortresses dated back to 600AD—amazing! They were fortresses, but they were also homes for some wealthy people. One's home served as a display of one's wealth and power. Inside the castle, they would store all their gold and jewels, making it truly important for this home to be impenetrable. My favorite thing was seeing the moats surrounding the castles. The moat usually contained alligators, and you only crossed the heavy-chained drawbridge with a secret password or handshake.

I'm not certain about the latter of those details, but they guarded their stuff well. In that day and age, people would storm the castle in order to get your riches, so you always had to be prepared. In today's day and age, 2020 and beyond, you still must be ready at all times. People won't usually storm your home to steal your riches, but they will tax you and sue you, and you may experience unforeseen stock market losses, etc. As I write this book, the entire world is experiencing the coronavirus/COVID-19 global pandemic, which is devastating the financial markets. There will always be problems that arise. The protection component of the model is designed to create maximum protection against things that will crush your hopes and dreams.

We never want to spend unnecessarily or be wasteful, but you must be emphatic when it comes to protecting your hopes and dreams. This is a time to be wise, not cheap. A wise person will prepare and be bulletproof against uncertainty.

> "By failing to prepare, you are preparing to fail."
> *- Benjamin Franklin*

Moving through the Model

AUTO/HOME INSURANCE

The goal here is to protect ourselves from a devastating life event that could cripple us financially. Obviously, both auto and home insurance are designed to protect our property in the event of an accident. Whether it is a fender-bender or a tree falling across our home, a good policy is designed to make us whole again.

There is a bigger purpose to these policies! They should be structured to protect all our assets and future income. Let me share a quick story with you to explain this further.

When you complete this book, you are so excited about all you've learned! In your exuberance, you head out to tell friends. As you leave your street, your cell phone falls out of the open window of your car. In your momentary distraction, you veer across the center line and hit someone and kill them. A horrible tragedy!

The person you killed happened to be just like you: 40 years old with an income of $100,000 per year with a wife and two children.

What happens next? Will the victim's wife/family sue you? If so, what will they sue you for? How much? Remember from the earlier chapter, the answer is, "As much as possible."

The courts have introduced a common calculation based upon someone's economic value. While the deceased may have been a great husband, father and person, many times the damages are limited to one's economic value.

Economic Value: The economic value of an individual is the amount calculated from one's yearly income, the income one gets leading to retirement, and other variables (savings, assets, etc.) to determine the financial loss a family will suffer in the case of a family member's death.

Economic value in our example:

Annual Income x Years Until Retirement = EV

$100,000 x 25 = 2,500,000

So, your "accident" has created a lawsuit of $2.5 million against you. Your insurance policy is now radically important in what it covers.

Most policies that I review state a coverage of 100/300. Meaning, in our example above, they will likely pay only $100,000 towards your $2.5M suit.

It is unlikely that an attorney will settle for $100k in this case. What next?

You would be required to pay from your assets (the ones which are NOT protected; more on this later) until you reach an agreement with the litigating party.

Wow! Talk about a major setback. Killing future hopes and dreams by giving up your savings and investments. Oh and by the way, if you didn't have enough assets to satisfy the claim, they could go after your future earnings.

> "We have to protect ourselves against massive life disruptions that kill our future hopes and dreams."
> - *Todd Burkhalter, CSA*

Please do not take me as being insensitive towards the gravity of this accident. The point of this story is to demonstrate the need for maximum protection. This same type of scenario holds true for our homeowners or renters policies. The need is for liability protection.

This liability protection is increased as you have children. During the early years of parenting, you will tend to have more of your children's friends over as well as the increased liability as your teen begins to drive.

Most insurance companies limit liability policies to 250/500 or $250,000 for a single accident or $500,000 for a multiple person claim. So what's the answer?

Umbrella Policy: Umbrella insurance refers to liability insurance that is in excess of specified other policies and also potentially primary insurance for losses not covered by the other policies.

When an insured is liable to someone, the insured's primary insurance policies pay up to their limits, and any additional amount is paid by the umbrella policy (up to the limit of the umbrella policy).

The great thing about these policies is they are generally super inexpensive. In our example above of the $2.5M lawsuit, if this person would have had a $2M umbrella policy in addition to their primary insurance, the suit would have likely been settled before reaching court and certainly before devastating their future incomes, assets, hopes and dreams.

These policies were just described as inexpensive. What do I mean? A $2,000,000 umbrella Policy costs roughly the amount of a really nice dinner out. Wait! You mean around $250 to $300 per year? That's right. Annual premiums for these policies are generally very affordable, within the few hundreds of dollars range per year, assuming you don't have extenuating circumstances, like hazardous extremes on your property.

Why wouldn't everyone have one of these types of policies? They absolutely should! This is where working with the proper team makes all the difference in the world. A good agent/advisor will mitigate risk for you. When you work off a 1-800 #, sadly you get what you get. An agent couldn't possibly make much money from selling a policy like this since the premiums are so low. From their standpoint, why take on the extra risk and paperwork for so little commission?

Insurance laws protect the consumer. Insurance cannot cost more for working with an agent. Use one who serves multiple highly rated companies and cares about your future.

Other Considerations: If you have adequate savings (easily accessible cash), you may consider raising your deductible (the amount you pay first before the insurance company begins to pay towards a claim). This may help to lower your premium (amount you pay for coverage). Maximum coverage is the first consideration!

Remember, this is the first line of defense from someone invading your castle. This is your moat, so make it as big as possible and put big alligators in it!

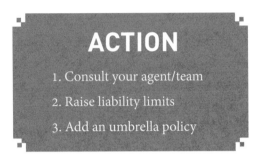

DISABILITY INCOME PROTECTION

You Are the Golden Goose

You may recognize this example of the goose versus the golden eggs. The one who provides income to their household, likely you if you're reading this book, is the golden goose, and your income is the golden eggs.

A person is more likely to become injured and be unable to work for 90 days than they are to die prematurely. Until you have income or cash flow that is NOT dependent upon your ability to get up and work, you will need to insure against this risk.

Action! Ask yourself: If I were to become sick, hurt and couldn't work, how long could I financially live? Based upon your answer, what would you sacrifice first? second? What bill wouldn't be paid first?

It is a potentially frightening question. In the coming pages, we will work towards strategies to provide us cash flow and income that isn't based upon our day-to-day activities. It is achieved through business or assets, like investments or properties paying us. Until then, let's make use of insurance.

Large companies often have disability income protection as an offered benefit. That is a benefit to take full advantage of; however, I would recommend working with an advisor to augment your coverage with a personally owned policy.

A personally owned policy (not related to your employer's plan) is important since it is portable and goes with you regardless if you were to separate employment. Separation of employment, whether from termination, quitting, etc., results in coverage going away.

You never want to have to work for someone else solely for benefits.

These types of policies are complex. Based upon the complexity, you are almost always forced to work with an expert in designing these types of income protection policies. The complexity ranges from coordinating it with any government or corporate benefits to how long benefits and determining how the actual benefit will be taxed. In addition, you will want to ensure that your policy is non-cancellable from the insurance company as well as the type of work you can do once you are beginning to heal.

The brevity in this section isn't due to a lack of importance or understanding. There are so many variables that will have to be discussed with an agent and with the underwriting team. My goal here is to impress upon you the importance of having this coverage properly structured until your cash flow is sufficient.

QUICK ACTION

1. Consult your agent/team
2. Maximize your disability income protection
3. Consider a policy that includes 401(k)/savings replacement
4. Aim for 80% to 90% of income replacement due to disability

HEALTH INSURANCE

If there was ever a section I'd love to skip, it would be this one. The ever-changing landscape of healthcare makes this one of the most difficult topics to advise upon. There are still salient points for you to consider in an effort to provide for you and your family and to keep your hopes and dreams/lifestyle design intact.

Health insurance for most healthy individuals and families should be used to cover the catastrophic events that would be financially devastating. Exceptions range from people with compromised health conditions or women who are likely to become pregnant.

Generally, we recommend health savings accounts (HSA) that provide a tax advantaged way to save for unexpected health issues or to cover your health insurance deductible (amount you pay before health insurance benefits begin to pay).

These plans have become costly due to the rising cost of healthcare and prescription medications. However, we also recommend analyzing the cost savings for becoming a self-pay patient. Self-pay patients often pay a mere fraction of the cost charged to insurance companies for the same procedure.

LONG-TERM CARE INSURANCE

When this comes up in conversations, we often think, *that is for old people*. This is kind of true. It is generally designed to take care of seniors when they need extended skilled care. First, let's define when it is typically used. There are 6 triggering events that dictate when this type of insurance could even be used if you own it.

THE 6 TRIGGERING EVENTS

1. Eating
2. Bathing
3. Getting Dressed
4. Toileting
5. Transferring
6. Continence

What are *triggering events*? They have to do with the 6 activities of daily living (ADLs). When someone can't perform approximately 3 of the ADLs listed or when cognitive abilities are diagnosed, LTC plans will begin to pay.

The reason I said "kind of true" above is because the need is typically for the elderly, but accidents, strokes or life events can make any of us susceptible to being unable to perform the ADLs described above. Therefore, we would need a plan like this since traditional healthcare phases out for long-term chronic illness.

These types of illnesses and healthcare conversations highlight the need for integrating all our planning into a cohesive plan that is well thought out and implemented.

Long-term care policies are often avoided due to the cost of the premium. In addition, many people are reluctant to purchase something that has a "only" a 50% chance of needing such a plan.

Insurance companies also recognize that healthcare costs are rising, and many policies have the right to increase your premiums as you age. It is scary to think you could pay and pay until you can't afford to pay.

Now, for the good news! I recommend structuring your long-term care so it literally costs you nothing. A properly structured life insurance policy can allow you to have a rider (additional benefit) that covers LTC at no additional cost.

There are only a few companies that offer such a benefit, but this one move will save you thousands of dollars and provide you the peace of mind you desire.

QUICK ACTION

1. This requires full-team coordination
2. Get an HSA and fund it
3. Get a policy for catastrophic coverage at a minimum
4. Consider being a self-pay patient
5. Coordinate your life insurance to cover long-term care

GOVERNMENT PLANS

A well-constructed financial plan or strategy that discusses lifestyle design should be dependent upon any type of government plan. One of the first government plans that comes to mind when you hear that phrase is Social Security.

When posed with the idea of Social Security, most Americans do not believe that it will be around for them. However, I actually disagree. Most economists agree that it will be around in some form. Let's talk about why and how this is possible, but more importantly, why it matters if we aren't planning on needing this government benefit.

NANNY'S STORY

My Grandmother, Nanny, lived with me in my childhood family home for most of my life. Before she went to be with Jesus at age 96, she received Social Security. During a conversation near the end of her life, she shared with me, "I got a raise!" Inquiring further, she shared that her Social Security income had increased. I replied, "Great news!" and we moved on quickly to one of her favorite subjects: Braves baseball.

Isn't it interesting that Social Security continues to provide raises even though the plan is under-funded and scheduled to run out of money? If you examine the facts, it is quite believable though because the plan/raises are determined by politicians.

Think about being the politician who kills Social Security. You wouldn't be a politician for long. The Baby Boomer generation is currently America's largest voting demographic. With this generation either already enjoying the SS benefit or poised to do so, it would be political suicide.

In fact, it has been proposed three times by our legislators to push the retirement time to age 70 1/2. While it hasn't passed yet, it appears only to be a matter of time for this to be a method of taking strain off the already beleaguered system. That is why I believe Social Security will be around for us all, but it will be the working population who will pay for the continued benefits.

A discussion of Social Security and its future still isn't the most relevant talking point as it relates to our personal finances and planning. Consider this: currently we are in the third-lowest income tax environment in the history of the United States. Even at the third-lowest tax rate ever, if asked, everyone believes they pay too much!

THE PROBLEM

The United States of America currently (2020) has a $23 trillion deficit. We fight wars all over, and currently, we are in the midst of a pandemic virus. We deal with corporate bail-outs and Homeland Security issues, Social Security is underfunded, we are building a wall, etc. These are only a few of the tugs on our money. We have many programs and groups bidding for government funds; some are good, and some are not so good.

Every economist agrees that we will likely see a Tax Rate Increase regardless of who is in office going forward.

So, allow me to pose this question to you:

Is it possible that we could experience higher tax rates in the future than we have today?

I suspect that most reasonable people would agree that it is not only possible but highly likely based upon the state of our government and country which we've discussed.

This potentially long-winded and exhaustive narrative is simply to say this: going forward, we must keep this in the forefront of our mind when planning for our future financial decisions.

Many plans that Americans and our American government favor are based around being taxed later. This means deferring our tax to a future date with a potentially higher and less favorable tax rate.

It makes more sense to search for tax-free investments and programs going forward.

WILLS AND DOCUMENTS

There are probably as many lawyer jokes as there are blonde jokes. Being married to a blonde, I'll say that the blondes don't deserve it.

Obviously, I am kidding. Attorneys provide a great service to families and businesses to ensure that assets are protected and are handled with the care we desire. It is an obligation as a parent, spouse, and an adult to have your will and healthcare directives completed. It's the proper and non-selfish thing to do.

A will is merely a legal document that states your assets and how you wish for them to be distributed at your death.

The stakes are raised when you have children. When you have children, you must also direct who the guardians of your children should be if you and their other parent die or aren't available. These are decisions you do not want a court-appointed person making on your behalf.

In previous chapters, we discussed the importance of coordinating our financial decisions. The will is frequently overlooked as a place for coordination. You will want to make sure you coordinate your beneficiaries with trusts in order to ensure the assets reach the desired beneficiary.

HEALTHCARE DIRECTIVES

Healthcare directives take the pressure off of family members when you are unable to make healthcare decisions for yourself. Unfortunately, I have been in both circumstances with families where there were directives in place and another where no direction was provided. The tension in either situation is high due to a loved one being in a serious medical situation. There is an added element of peace when families are "taken off the hook" from having to make such huge decisions on their own. Get them done!

DISASTER FILE

In a life-or-death situation, wouldn't it be great to have five more minutes with the person whom you love the most? It would be a gift that both would cherish forever.

During the terrorist attacks of 9/11, many individuals had a chance to make one last call. Many left voice messages or actually got through to family members, and I suspect that none of them wasted those few last minutes discussing how to spend money or where certain accounts or passwords were held. It was a time only used to express their love, as it should have been.

I use that example to set the stage for creating a disaster file. When plans do not work out as expected, or when you don't make it home one night, this document will provide additional valuable information about important matters and even some love notes.

This is a best-practices concept I've used for years, and I hope this book gives you inspiration to create such a useful and thoughtful tool.

TRUSTS AND OWNERSHIP

Trusts and corporate structures are often deemed as something only the ultra-wealthy would own. This is a common misconception for many people getting started. As mentioned above, these are simply tools that ensure asset protection.

Recall our story about the auto accident? In that example, when the person didn't have enough insurance coverage and the victim's attorney went rifling through their assets, these tools would have been super helpful for the plaintiff to keep their assets.

Trusts and limited liability companies (LLC) are ways to own certain assets like real estate, businesses or accounts. This is important because an LLC or a trust doesn't drive a car or say dumb things like people often do. Therefore, in many circumstances, using tools like these can help to avoid losing assets due to litigation or at least to minimize the damage.

THINGS TO CONSIDER

- Never personally own investment real estate
- Use trusts as beneficiaries for life insurance and other investment accounts
- Consider owning investments in a corporate entity when possible

LIFE INSURANCE

Life insurance is a financial tool; when designed correctly, it can provide numerous benefits. At the core, life insurance is designed to replace the insured's income or assets at their death.

There are two initial questions that should be answered when discussing life insurance.

1. How much life insurance should I own?
2. What type of life insurance should I own?

HOW MUCH LIFE INSURANCE SHOULD I OWN?

Hopefully, you recall our standard answer from Chapter 4:

As much as possible!

I'm certainly not a schill for the insurance industry, but I have delivered several death claim checks across my career. Never, not once, did the beneficiary say, "No thanks," or "That's way too much." More often it was greeted with, "Thank God; this will be a huge help."

You should always aim to have your full economic value in insurance whenever possible. Having your EV in life insurance guarantees that the hopes and dreams you have for your family are fulfilled, whether you work your full career or if you die before you reach the end of your working years.

Remember: your economic value is your annual income x # of working years. Once you reach retirement or when you have cash flow to provide your income, the EV calculation shifts to equal the value of your assets.

WHAT TYPE OF LIFE INSURANCE SHOULD I OWN?

Like many other financial tools, there are different types of plans available for life insurance, but generally there are two basic types: term insurance and permanent insurance. As we've discussed previously, this is also one of those critical questions that should be addressed by your financial team as a whole. There are many products and complexities within each type that should be considered. Together, we will explore the basics in design and recommendations.

Term Life Insurance: Just as the name indicates, this type of coverage insures your life for a term or period of time. At the end of that period, the plan will terminate or expire without value.

Permanent Life Insurance: Just as the name indicates, this type of coverage insures your life until the end of your life. This type of coverage allows for a portion of the premium to accumulate within the policy, creating cash value that can be accessed by the policy owner.

An easy way to differentiate between the two types of coverage is to use the analogy of a home. Term life insurance would be like renting the coverage for a time frame, whereas permanent coverage is more closely related to owning where you actually build up equity inside the plan.

The obvious choice for many would be to avoid wasting money on term insurance, if it is like renting, since we know that roughly 99% of these policies never actually pay out a claim. Most individuals live beyond the terms of the plan, which is obviously a good thing. You'd never want to have to die in order to win with any plan.

Permanent insurance is the best way to go for anyone who plans to save or invest money for 10 years. Continuing to make your premium payments into well-structured policies will allow for a buildup of cash value. The cash value of these plans are excellent places to create emergency reserves and opportunity funds. The cash value enjoys accessibility, tax-free growth and creditor protection. The internal cash in these plans allow for it to be invested in the general assets of the insurance company or to track along with several stock market indices. This is a great way to enjoy the benefits of the stock market yet enjoy no loss provisions offered through the insurance companies.

Some individuals with lower savings rates will use term insurance due to the lower premium outlay. In these cases, we recommend making sure that the insured has a "conversion clause" for all or most of the duration of the policy. This conversion clause allows for a policy to be converted into a permanent policy without having to re-qualify medically. We always say that insurance policies are bought with your money and your health. Therefore, the educated consumer would never keep a term life policy beyond their conversion period.

Owning permanent coverage or maintaining the ability to convert your term policy ensures that you will have coverage throughout your entire life. As a financial planner, this is helpful when developing traditional retirement income strategies. Having a properly structured policy during your senior years allows you to maintain the additional features of long-term care, maximum income opportunity from retirement plans as well as estate and legacy-planning options.

QUICK ACTION

- Secure your economic value in life insurance
- Ensure that it has a long conversion clause
- Permanent insurance provides the most benefits

FINAL THOUGHTS

The protection component, when well designed, will bring you the freedom to live a rich, full life and it will give you a real sense of peace. Hopefully, you picked up some good ideas and best practices from this section. As I have stressed, this should all be done and coordinated within your overall plans by a team of professionals.

Growing up in Atlanta as a baseball fan, everyone loved the longtime voice of the Atlanta Braves, Skip Carey. As the late innings of a tight scoring ballgame approached, Skip was notorious for saying, "We sure could use a little insurance right now!" Of course he was describing the need for some extra runs to provide a bigger cushion in the game. I believe that is what most people really want in life: a larger cushion or increased security. This is why the castles we discussed earlier created those large moats.

YOU NEVER WANT TO HAVE TO WORK FOR SOMEONE ELSE SOLELY FOR BENEFITS

CHAPTER 6

SAVINGS

Many of us have been taught from an early age to save. We've been told things like "A penny saved is a penny earned." I believe that our parents and Benjamin Franklin meant well, but they should have at some point interchanged the word *save* with *invest*. I mention Benjamin Franklin only because he is attributed with most quotes related to saving. Don't get me wrong, it is a good thing to save, but I believe that we should redefine when, where and how we save.

The first steps in saving should be to protect against the most immediate problems that could arise. Simply providing for the most immediate of emergencies will prevent you from having to run to credit cards or other loans that could continue to haunt you for a long time.

There is a lot of financial pornography that is circulated throughout the world. I refer to it as pornography because if followed, it will often times lead to you into trouble. Popular financial magazines have allowed their ad sponsors to influence their content. Typical content directs most Americans towards financial products offered by sponsor companies, regardless if it is in the best interest of the consumer.

The government, as well as these publications, have sold the idea to the American public that they should max out retirement plans as one of the first moves in someone's career. As we've seen on the Protection Savings and Growth Model, there are a number of steps that proceed the funding of long-term retirement plans, which as we know could be tax traps for us down the road.

Let's discuss some of the best practices and steps to take in the savings component of the model. Most people avoid subjects they do not fully understand. As a result, when someone hasn't taken the time to become financially educated, they are apt to take no action whatsoever. This is a potential disaster if continued for long periods of time. Therefore, as a first step, we recommend establishing a wealth coordination account or WCA. Before you begin searching the web for the best WCA, you will not find it. This was a phrase that was developed internally, and we didn't consult Google.

A wealth coordination account is a place (e.g., a savings or checking account that is separate from all others) where someone can place their 15% savings even when they aren't fully certain of exactly where it should go. Having this outlet allows you to have certainty in your steps as well as to avoid periods where you skip saving all together. Over the years, an unintended consequence has been that the WCA serves as a nice audit trail once you begin allocating those funds to different areas of the model.

As your WCA expands, you will want to use those funds to build up 6 to 12 months of expenses as an emergency reserve. An emergency reserve is funds that are easily accessible and not impacted by market volatility. This money must be available, as stated earlier, for those unexpected problems that occur. A trip to Vegas or a concert does not constitute an emergency.

Once we have achieved an adequate emergency reserve fund, we can then start to develop our cash value within our life insurance plans. Over time, I believe this should ultimately serve as our emergency reserve fund. This process is a little slower to build, which is why we don't start there first. Properly structuring this as our emergency reserve will allow us to earn a better return on these funds and still maintain access and even greater security of the account.

Completing the steps above will provide you with freedom to begin investing. Investing to impact your lifestyle design and your hopes and dreams will mean that you will do things differently than many of your friends and colleagues.

> ## "Live like no one else,
> ## so that you can live like no one else." - *Dave Ramsey*

A natural step for many who have achieved the steps above would most likely begin with traditional retirement plans. I am referring to IRAs, ROTH IRAs, 401(k), Keogh plans, SEP plans and more. Before you think that I am bashing these popular plans, I am not—well, not really. One issue s I have for plans of this nature is that many defer tax until a later date, which could be detrimental. However, the larger issue, that I identify, is that it takes away money from your lifestyle today so that you can enjoy it later—way later for many of us. In our quest for lifestyle design, let's shoot for some of the same features that these traditional plans offer us in the future but search for a radical increase in the benefits we enjoy now. More clearly put: we can have tax advantages now, and income in the future and now. Sound too good to be true? It isn't.

THE GREAT MULTIPLIER

In the past, as you've approached investing your money, have you ever wondered what is the very best place to invest? Of course, most everyone has faced that challenge. The process of investing could be simplified if we didn't have to approach this question as an either/or scenario. For example, what if we could invest into multiple things at one time? Problem solved.

Many traditional plans don't afford the luxury of each dollar being utilized simultaneously in different markets. One tool within the savings component allows for this multiplier effect of each dollar being able to receive multiple rates of return at the same time. I am referring to one of our earlier moves that provided cash value from the life insurance that we implemented in an earlier chapter. The cash value from permanent life insurance shows up in the tax-free box of the PS&G Model. When properly structured, life insurance cash value participates in the gains of the stock market. The insurance company allows the policy owner a loan provision, using the cash value as collateral. This loan allows the full value of the cash to stay invested as well as the freedom to use up to 90% of the CV elsewhere on the PS&G Model, preferably within the growth component to create cash flow/income.

When this advanced concept is initially introduced, there is a tendency to say, "Whoa! I don't feel that I should have to loan myself my own money!" You're technically not. The insurance company is sending their money for the loan and your money is serving as collateral for such a loan. This is what allows the cash value to continue to grow in an uninterrupted manner within the policy.

This move allows our money to work double- and triple-duty when you look at the overall return. This return is multiplied further when you factor in the potential tax advantages of certain investments and tax deductions of the overall strategy.

QUICK ACTIONS

- Create a wealth coordination account
- Fund 15% of your gross (before-tax) income
- Have emergency reserves of 6 to 12 months of your household income
- Begin creating cash value through permanent life insurance

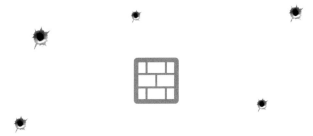

CHAPTER 7

BULLETPROOF YOUR WEALTH

B ulletproof anything sounds pretty cool to me. It conjures up images of a Mad Max-style vehicle rolling through a city doing as they wish. A more refined vision would be the President of the United States safely inside his state car, with a bulletproof motorcade. Either example exudes a cool yet tough feel of being invisible. Wouldn't it be great to have that same feeling when it comes to your personal finances? Do you have that feeling about your current plans? What are some of the attributes of a bulletproof set of financial plans?

- Predictable growth/high growth rate
- Tax rates fixed or tax-free
- Not market-based or volatile
- Provides income now
- Protected from lawsuits
- Continues if disabled
- Self-complete in case of a premature death
- Plan is easy to understand and flexible

That would be a good list if you could make investments that achieved some or all of the attributes above. While not always possible to achieve 100% of the above, it is possible to get close when you combine strategies and tools. Before we advance into the next chapter, where we look at the growth component of the Protection Savings and Growth Model, I want to introduce a new lens or filter for examining your investment opportunities.

As you approach new investments, or as you examine existing plans, ask yourself, what type of wealth is this building? Would this be categorized as statement wealth or contractual wealth? Let's examine the two types of wealth.

STATEMENT WEALTH

Imagine yourself walking towards your mailbox or logging into an online portal to receive a statement from a bank, a credit union, an investment company, a mutual fund or a retirement plan. When you get the statement, you look at the balance, which makes you either happy, sad, indifferent or maybe even confused. The question that comes to mind is, how much control did you have over the outcome and how was it taxed? While you certainly, or likely, chose the investment or account, you still didn't have much control over the end result. They simply sent you a statement to share with you how it turned out.

CONTRACTUAL WEALTH

Contractual wealth indicates that there is a contract in place. When someone enters into a contract, they typically have negotiated or agreed to some terms of a deal. Therefore, this type of wealth frankly requires a bit more thought to the process, which is possibly why most people never fully achieve this style of wealth. A contract says to me that if I do my part, then another party has some obligation or skin in the game to fulfill our deal. This idea of skin in the game means that if things do not work out as planned, then you as a party to the contract have recourse or rights.

As we did earlier, imagine you opening that statement that we mentioned above. Upon opening your statement, you see that ABC Fund Company is reporting that you lost 50% of your account's value due to a correction or market event. Now, envision yourself calling the ABC Fund Company and suggesting that they refund you the 50% that you lost! That call would likely be laughable, right?

This example of statement wealth seems extreme, but it is meant highlight that in many investments, you have no recourse or control.

Having contractual wealth offers a more predictable path to Designing the Life you desire. This type of wealth typically allows for greater control of returns and taxation thus creating a greater sense of peace during turbulent times. So, as you examine new or old opportunities think through this concept of statement versus contractual wealth. Contractual wealth provides that feeling of bulletproof that we love for our members.

CHAPTER 8

GROWTH

Ahh, finally we get to the good stuff! This is what most people enjoy discussing: stocks, bonds and real estate. Anxious to build their castle and to create wealth, many people overlook building the moat, which protects them from outside looting and pillaging. It feels good for a while, but the neglect will ultimately catch up to you at some point. So, you can't skip the previous steps!

Jumping to this area of finances first is simple for many; frankly, it is sexier and much cooler to discuss at cocktail parties. Have you ever heard someone bragging over drinks about their prowess for picking insurance or navigating the savings account market? Of course not!

This is the last step in a loop or continuum of creating bulletproof finances we desire. Using the proper tools within the growth component, if done correctly, should allow you to begin augmenting the income you receive from your primary occupation. Augmenting your income helps you to enjoy luxuries and experiences that others may not be able to afford, but the ultimate goal for many is to fully replace your income through the cash flow from these investments.

Traditional planning or your parents' style of planning usually involved investing into stocks and bonds but never touching them in an effort to accumulate enough that one day, in "retirement," they could enjoy their delayed gratification. This approach flips that script to suggest you can reach that goal much sooner than the timeframe dictated by Social Security and retirement plan rules and timelines. Sound good? Let's get into how it's done.

In lieu of strictly sticking to stocks and bonds, we prefer to use a more contractual wealth-driven approach. This approach will use three primary avenues ideally funded through utilizing our permanent insurance policies or other cash flow from our wealth coordination account (WCA). The three primary tools are private contractual agreements, real estate and businesses.

PRIVATE CONTRACTUAL AGREEMENTS

Private contractual agreements are deals that are made between you and a business owner or company that is looking for partners to help them grow. Often times, this could mean that you gain income from lending your money or expertise to an opportunity. These types of deals are all around you, but most people's networks never discuss opportunities like these. This is why we recommend you surround yourself with a team who will frequently expose you to new opportunities. There are also companies that can guide you to other entrepreneurs seeking these partnerships. Usually, these types of investments are taxed at the best rates and provide an above-average return. Since this is well within our contractual wealth parameters, these types of agreements will often come with ownership or other rights of control.

> "Your income will be the average
> of your top five friends." - *Grant Cardone*

REAL ESTATE

Real estate is responsible for more millionaires than any other type of investment. You may have even heard people suggest investing in real estate because they aren't creating any more of it! While there is truth in both statements, let's be specific about the type of real estate investing that we're talking about here. We want to purchase real estate that provides cash flow now. Here are some common mistakes that a novice will make when it comes to real estate:

- Thinking your home as an investment
- Purchasing land or properties that do not create income
- Overpaying for property
- Improper financing of real estate

When designing your life, I usually want to start with investing into property that you and others will always desire to visit. This means that you can create income from properties that you absolutely love. Think mountain home, beach home, etc. These short-term rental properties can be owned inside of an LLC for asset protection while creating significant tax advantages and income. The coup de grace of this strategy is that you're creating a beautiful life of traveling to visit your destination properties.

The next type of real estate to consider is multi-family housing. This would constitute duplex, triplex and apartments. These multi-family units are reliable investments that offer significant tax advantages plus the security of large numbers. When you own a lot of different units, you spread the risk out over many families/tenants as opposed to owning a single-family home, which is reliant only on that single tenant. This type of real estate investment is said to be recession-proof because even in poor economies, people will still need a home.

Lastly, it is easier to gain financing for real estate since the property can serve as its own collateral. Therefore, you can use leverage to create cash flow without using a significant portion of your own money as a down payment. Ideally and whenever possible, we use the permanent life insurance's cash value strategy for loaning yourself the down payment, thus allowing those funds to remain invested in the market-based account as well as creating cash flow from the short-term rental property or multi-family unit.

BUSINESS

Just second to real estate in the hierarchy of millionaires is business owners. In the past, owning a business was something that only few wealthy people could afford. The advancement of the internet and other technology has led us to a new type of economy and business models. With the gig economy, people can more easily market and utilize their skill sets for profit. Between the gig economy and the sharing economies, such as Uber, Airbnb and many others, it has never been easier to open a business.

Business ownership however isn't for the faint of heart. An entrepreneur has to be mentally, emotionally and financially tough. Owning a business has the capacity to run your life, and that can be either good or bad. Personally, I have been my own boss for most all of my career, and I do not want to paint a bad picture here. I simply want to emphasize that there are good and bad ways to run a business.

When owning your own business, we stress that you begin as quickly as possible to create a focus on "the big four." The big Four are the keys to any business, large or small. Whether you're the size of Coca-Cola or a mom-and-pop shop, the basic rules are the same. There must be focused metrics on marketing, human capital (employees), business real estate and financials. Owning a business puts you at the helm of your future. It is liberating and at times bulletproof.

QUICK ACTION

- Use contractual wealth tools for cash flow
- Identify potential real estate that you will love to visit
- Identify your skills and passions as a potential business

CHAPTER 9

WHAT ABOUT THE STOCK MARKET?

For all of the bulls and bears out there, I haven't forgotten about you. Stocks, bonds, ETFs and mutual funds certainly fall within the growth component, which we discussed in Chapter 8. The markets are additional ways for someone to create wealth, but unfortunately, it almost always lends itself to statement wealth. Most individuals do not have the education, training or discipline to manage their own stock and bond portfolios. For those who have market-based plans already, what do you do? Our recommendation: turn it over to the professionals.

MUTUAL FUNDS AND EXCHANGE]TRADED FUNDS

Mutual funds and exchange-traded funds are portfolios (or baskets) of individual companies' stocks or bonds. This method allows for a professional money manager to choose when and which companies to buy and sell. This takes the pressure off the individual to do the research but also spreads the risk out among numerous investments. For beginning investors and smaller account balances, these are reasonable options to get started.

I would like to suggest that exchange-traded funds are a superior option to mutual funds when considering using this method of investing. Mutual funds have additional fees within them that exchange-traded funds (ETF) do not. In addition, there are features related to pricing that provide the investor to get in or out of the investment during volatile markets, thus making this a safer option for investors. Albeit noted as safer, I still do not believe that most individuals should choose this route.

INDIVIDUAL STOCKS AND BONDS PORTFOLIOS

This is the preferred method of investing into these markets: individual positions/ investments that are managed in a disciplined manner. It is critical to do your research to find the right manager. Only managers who are set up to hedge or to mitigate risk within the portfolio should get your attention. These hedging strategies are sophisticated methods of using puts, calls straddles and more. Hedging allows for an investor to lower their risk and ideally make money regardless if the stock market increases or decreases. These technical moves definitely should be handled by firms with the proper structure to manage them. As I mentioned, this is the only way that I recommend significant wealth be invested into the market but only after the other facets of the PS&G Model have been perfected.

QUICK ACTION

For old 401(K)s or IRA plans, choose a managed account with either an ETF or an individually managed account with hedge strategies. This is based on account value and desire to invest in the stocks and bonds markets.

CHAPTER 10

WHAT'S NEXT?

Bulletproof Your Finances is a bold title. You may even question if that is even possible. I will suggest that if you follow the methodology that has been laid out within this book, you will feel confident about your personal finances. There will be a tendency to skip steps, but please do not. Personal finances are most successful when done as a team sport. There will be tendency to try and go it alone, but please do not. Feeling confident or bulletproof is great, but there has to be more to it than just a feeling of confidence. There is absolutely more.

The "more" that I describe is within the concept of lifestyle design. I can't overstate enough the statement that if you don't design your life, someone will do it for you. I promise. You must take the time to dream big and to follow the steps to creating the cash flow or income that allows you to live freely. Please do not think that I am indicating that money solves all your problems. It doesn't. Having income does ease certain pressures that exist in life. Part of your design should also include a strategic approach towards your relationships and health, which we identify as the remaining two elements of true success.

Go enjoy life, live large and impact those you encounter.

Made in the USA
Columbia, SC
19 November 2023

26740154R00024